AWS

CERTIFIED CLOUD PRACTITIONER

*AWS Cloud Practitioner Ultimate
Cheatsheet, Practice Test Questions with
Detailed Explanations and Links*

HILLARY MORRISON

TABLE OF CONTENTS

Introduction

The Amazon Web Services Cloud Computing Certification (AWS CCP or CCP) is a great introductory course. It is the pathway exam into the other AWS Certifications such as the Solution Architect Associate (SAA) course.

There are no prerequisites for the course but it is advisable to have some basic knowledge of technology or cloud computing experience. Your experience in information technology or cloud computing will determine the approximate hours you will need to prepare for the exam. This could be anywhere from 8-hours to 40-hours (2-weeks).

The AWS CCP course and exam is the foundation course for learning AWS. It is also unique in that it is one of the few AWS courses to explain the business-centric along with the billing concepts of AWS.

Even though it is not a certification that will give you much of a boost on your resume, it is a course that even the top developers involved in any form of cloud computing should take. AWS CCP is also an excellent course for all levels of management from mid-level, right up to CEO or VPs to take. It is the basis of how AWS Cloud Computing works and it is definitely a must-have certification for any salesperson involved with AWS or cloud computing.

Being able to master and navigate the way information technology test center exams work is a great confidence booster. Especially for those looking to continue the AWS certification path as all the testing facilities are very similar except for practical lab type environments. The CCP is an exam or certificate that helps you ease into the AWS certification path as it is not a very hard exam to take.

Chapter 1

AWS Certified Cloud Practitioner

The CCP is the first step to the AWS Solution Architect Associate certification and has some information that works as the foundation for the SAA. It is not too expensive and it is one of the best entry-level exams to take in order to help you with the harder exams.

What Students Need to Know for the Exam

The AWS Certified Cloud Practitioner exam is divided into four domains which are:

Domain 1 — Cloud Concepts

Domain 1, which is cloud concepts, accounts for 26% of the CCP exam.

The exam covers the following topics:

- What is AWS and its value propositions?

- What are the advantages of AWS Cloud?

- AWS Core Services

- Architecture Design Principles of the Cloud

Domain 2 — Security

Domain 2, which is AWS Security, accounts for 25% of the CCP exam.

This section covers the following topics:
- Shared Responsibility Model

- Cloud Security and Compliance

- Access Management Capabilities

- Security Support Resources

Domain 3 — Technology

Domain 3, which is technology, is the biggest section of the exam and accounts for 33% of the CCP exam.

Technology covers the following topics:

- Overview of methods for deploying and operating in the AWS Cloud

- Overview of the AWS global infrastructure

- AWS Core services

- Technology support resources

Domain 4 — Billing and Pricing

Domain 4, which is the billing and pricing, which is an important part of AWS, accounts for 16% of the CCP exam.

Billing and Pricing cover the following topics:

- AWS pricing models

- AWS billing and pricing account structures

- Billing resources support

AWS Course and Exam Resources

The AWS CCP course white papers are available from the AWS website. You can create an account at the https://www.aws.training/ website or you can use an Amazon.com user id if you already have one.

Once you have logged on to the website you will have a host of resources available to you which include:

- Learning Library

- Certification Library

- AWS Training and Certification Portal Support

- Partner Training Information

You can register for the AWS Cloud Practitioner course and get the course white papers needed to ready you to take the certification exam.

This portal also has resources such as a training overview, learning paths, and exam study guide, plus test questions that can all be downloaded. There are also exam preparation webinars and support groups you can join to help to prepare for the exam.

The exam can be taken at a registered test center or as a proctored exam; this is covered in more detail in Chapter 6 of this book. The AWS Training website does have practice exams that can be taken, although there is a charge for them. The price of the practice exams can be found on the above-mentioned website.

The following website is a handy resource:

https://aws.amazon.com/certification/certification-prep/

This website page will give you access to AWS white paper, FAQ's, sample questions, exam readiness tests; there is also a link to get you set up to take a practice exam. Additionally, look for the link on the page where you can schedule the CCP exam.

Benefits of Becoming an AWS Certified Cloud Practitioner

Many advanced developers tend to want to skip over the AWS CCP exam but in actuality it is quite a handy certification to have. Other than being able to show you have an understanding of AWS, you also get access to a private AWS LinkedIn page, and access to various access codes for the AWS Certified Store. The more AWS exams you pass the more code accesses you will receive.

For companies with certified AWS employees it helps to cut down on risk when implementing AWS solutions having trained AWS employees. It also offers a higher tier access to the AWS Partner Networks (APN), which can be beneficial to some businesses.

Chapter 2

Cloud Concepts

These include cloud computing concepts and the AWS global infrastructure, which are covered in this chapter, along with getting started with AWS.

Cloud Computing Concepts

One of the most important questions that a person needs to understand before learning about AWS is:

What is Cloud Computing?

Cloud computing is the practice of using a network of servers that are remotely hosted on the internet in place of using locally hosted servers or a local system to manage, store, process, and share data or resources.

Cloud computing uses cloud providers which means:

- That the cloud provider is responsible for maintaining the hardware and software.

- That the cloud provider is responsible for the hiring of IT staff to manage and run the systems.

- That the cloud provider is responsible for renting or owning the property where the data centers are housed.

- The cloud provider is responsible for all the risks associated with the running, managing, and maintaining systems.

- That the customer is only responsible for configuring and maintaining their cloud or any code used by them.

On-premise computing means:

- That an organization owns or leases its equipment which includes servers and other networking systems.

- That an organization is responsible for the hiring of their IT staff to manage, run, and maintain the on-premise systems.

- That an organization takes on all the risks involved with the running, maintenance, and management of the on-premise systems.

- That any data centers or buildings housing the on-premise systems are owned, rented, or leased by an organization.

Large corporations tend to have on-premise computing systems although some are finding it beneficial to move some if not all of their systems to cloud-based computing systems. For small to medium-sized businesses, cloud computing definitely has its benefits and offers greater opportunities for better and more advanced systems that are cost-effective.

The Advantages of Cloud Computing

There are many advantages and benefits for businesses as well as individuals to use cloud computing services.

These advantages and benefits include:

On-Demand Resources

Instead of investing in on-premise solutions that can cost a fortune for the initial outlay, cloud services allow for pay-on demand services. This means that the cost of buying expensive servers and software to run on the servers is completely cut out. Instead, the company only pays for the resources it uses. The facility allows customers to get what they want when they want without having to wait for resources.

Pay as You Go

With on-demand resources, the customer is only paying for what they need or use. This eliminates long-term commitments and allows for resources that the company no longer needs to do away with the resources.

When IT managers scope out systems they do so by calculating how much data on average the organization uses over a span of two years or so. With that in mind, they need to make an estimate as to what a system will require to incorporate company growth for the next few years. As data usage within an organization can grow, stagnate, or even slow down this is mostly prediction analysis. With cloud computing, there is no more guesswork or having to upgrade the system every two years or so to ensure the company does not run out of space. With cloud computing services there is no paying for underutilized capacity or running out of capacity; the system can be scaled up or down as or when required.

Cost Sharing

Because other customers are using cloud services, cloud service providers can offer better deals to their customers. In essence this means that you are sharing the cost of data centers, software, and resources with other users of the cloud.

Greater Agility and Increased Speed

Not only can you scale solutions on-demand, but any new software roll-outs or upgrades can be done from one central location. This can also be done in a matter of minutes instead of having lengthy roll-outs that can take months if not years to deploy depending on the size of the on-premise network.

No More Data Center Costs

Cut down on expensive data centers or regulation server rooms. This allows for an organization to invest more on desktop systems rather than expensive server solutions.

Managed Services

AWS offers managed services, which frees an organization up to use the tool instead of having the operational burdens of managing the tools.

Expand Nationally or Globally

Expanding globally or nationally no longer requires having to invest in expensive resources. Organizations can now run their applications(s) from the cloud, enabling their staff to work from anywhere in the world with ease.

AWS Value Propositions

The advantages of implementing AWS offer the customer the following benefits:

- OpEx over CapEx means that there is more cash flow and a better bottom line for the customer.

- Agility and flexibility allowing for on-demand resources that are not readily available for on-premise systems. It also gives the customer more choice of applications or systems that was not possible in an on-premise system environment.

- Scalability is fast and can be done in a matter of minutes saving time, resources, and money. This elasticity gives customers room for growth that on-premise systems may have either a limit to or is too costly.

- Time to market is decreased due to not having lengthy system roll-outs, getting large budgets passed for the cost of equipment, resources, etc.

- Security of the AWS Cloud computing system gives customers peace of mind. There is no need for large backup centers, it eliminates downtime, and off-site disaster recovery centers.

The Types of Cloud Computing

There are different types of cloud computing available for use. These are chosen depending on the organization's needs.

Types of cloud computing include:

Software as a Service (SaaS)

Software as a Service are customer orientated services that provide software that is a whole product. In other words, it does not need any tweaks or developing it just works and is maintained by the provider of the service.

Some examples of SaaS include; Gmail, Salesforce, Google Apps, Zendesk, DocuSign, Dropbox, Slack, Monday.com, and MS Office 365.

Platform as a Service (PaaS)

Platform as a Service provides fully managed and maintained infrastructure for developers. The service provider will provide the hardware and already installed software so developers can concentrate on the development and deployment of their applications.

Some examples of PaaS include; Microsoft, Google, IBM, AWS, Red Hat, Pivotal, Oracle, Heroku, Mendix, AWS Elastic Beanstalk, and Engine Yard.

Infrastructure as a Service (IaaS)

Infrastructure as a Service is the infrastructure backbone that provides scalable solutions to meet a customer's cloud computing needs. This is where the storage solutions, processing services, and computers are provided for a customer's use. IaaS targets IT, administrative users, as a basic to more advanced knowledge in IT is needed to manage these services.

Services offered with IaaS can include; firewalls, auto-scaling, load balancers, monitoring, computing, databases, storage, content delivery networks, and more.

Some examples of IaaS include; Microsoft Azure, Google Cloud Platform, and AWS.

Deployment Methods for Cloud Computing

There are a few basic methods of deployment for cloud computing which include the following.

Public Cloud

The public cloud is the most widely used cloud and is the cloud that most people think of when the term cloud computing is mentioned. This is where everything that is used is owned, managed, and run by a third party. Here all the resources and services are provided over the public internet and are the cheapest of all deployment methods as it is paid on a per user basis.

The downfall of this deployment method is that it leaves an establishment or person totally reliant on the third party for its services. If the third party has an outage or interruption it is going to affect these services.

An example of this deployment method would include DropBox, Google Drive, Square Space, BaseCamp, and Slack.

This is the best platform to use for internet-based companies, start-ups, and is the basis for SaaS offerings.

Private Cloud

A private cloud is not shared by other companies or individuals, it is owned or leased by the organization or individual. A private cloud is usually intranet-based which means the only way to gain access to it is through the company network or a VPN application.

Although this type of cloud solution is just as flexible as the public cloud and offers the same sort of benefits as the public cloud it is more secure. Access is limited to a company or person with user access to it.

The major downfall of a private cloud is the cost of the cloud solution and as such, it is mostly used by large corporations or companies with the budget for it.

Community Cloud

The community cloud is much like the public cloud mixed with the private cloud. This type of deployment method allows for software and systems to be maintained by the service provider with shared resources between several organizations. The community cloud can be either maintained independently by the organization or the cloud provider. This type of cloud deployment is flexible, scalable, and offers the benefits of shared licenses, software, and other computing resources.

Although not nearly as expensive as the private cloud deployment method, the community cloud method can still be quite expensive to maintain. This deployment method best suits organizations such as manufacturing and financial institutes.

Hybrid Cloud

The hybrid cloud deployment method is one that can combine on-premise computing with one of the above cloud computing deployment methods. Or it can be the combination of the above-mentioned deployment methods.

Although this method can get messy in that it can create inconsistencies when it comes to the adherence of company policies, upgrades, maintenance, or software, a lot of larger corporations find it effective. This kind of deployment method allows for an organization to have flexible scalable solutions that meet its software and systems needs. They can also keep their more sensitive data on-site and secure it on their premises.

AWS Global Infrastructure

The previous section of this chapter gave you a basic understanding of cloud computing. It also introduced you to the different types of cloud computing, and the different deployment methods of cloud computing. This section of Chapter 2 will look at the AWS global infrastructure.

AWS has more than a million active customers that span the globe in over 190 different countries. In order to give AWS customers the most streamlined service that allows for a higher throughput while maintaining a lower latency Amazon continues to expand its global reach.

You can see the AWS Global Infrastructure at the following website link:

https://www.infrastructure.aws/

AWS Global Infrastructure is broken into:

Regions

As of the publishing of this guide, AWS could be found in 24 launched geographic locations around the globe. The region being where AWS is physically located around the world. Each region is a completely independent entity to any another region.

Each geographical region will have at least two independent data centers (availability zones or AZs) with the largest of the regions being North Virginia or the US-East.

Most of the new AWS services always first become available within the US-East region. All billing information is run from US-East 1 and it is important to note that not all services are available in all the regions.

AWS Regions include the following geographic locations:

Asia Pacific

- Beijing
- Hong Kong SAR

- Mumbai

- Seoul

- Singapore

- Sydney

- Tokyo

- Osaka

Europe / Middle East /Africa

- Frankfurt

- Ireland

- London

- Milan

- Paris

- Stockholm

- Bahrain

- Cape Town

North America

- AWS GovCloud (US-EAST)

- AWS GovCloud (US-WEST)

- Canada Central

- Northern California

- North Virginia (US-EAST)

- Ohio

- Oregon

South America

- São Paulo

To see all the current regions you can go to the AWS website; following the link below will take you directly to the page:

https://aws.amazon.com/about-aws/global-infrastructure/?p=ngi&loc=0

Scroll down the page to the world map. If you click on each continent it will bring up a list of all the current Regions, Availability Zones, Edge Locations, Regional Edge Locations, and Local Regions.

These can also be referenced on the AWS website. For more detailed information, go to:

https://aws.amazon.com/about-aws/global-infrastructure/regions_az/?p=ngi&loc=2

Availability Zones (AZ)

As of the publishing of this guide, AWS had 69 availability zones which are discrete data centers housed in the 24 geographic locations throughout the world.

An availability zone (AZ) is a discrete data center and there are usually two or more AZs per region. AZs that are found in the same region are completely isolated, separated, and independent of each other. They are designed to be independent failure zones that are only connected through fast, low latency, and redundant links. Every AZ is redundantly connected to multiple tier-1 transit providers. Each individual AZ is fed off a different grid from an independent facility. The sites all have onsite backup generation systems and a discreet UPS.

Customers can choose their availability or allow AWS to find the best ones for them according to their specific needs and requirements. AZs can be identified by a region code and letter identifier, for instance, US-WEST-1a. The AZ ID is the unique identifier for an AZ and is what a customer should use to coordinate AZs across accounts.

To see a list of availability zones (AZs) following the links referenced under the *"Regions"* section of this chapter (above).

Edge Locations
Edge locations are data centers that are owned and or operated by trusted AWS partners or affiliates. They are CloudFront Content Delivery Network (CDN) endpoints; there are more edge locations around the globe than there are regions. As of publishing this

guide, there were over 205 edge locations and 11 regional edge caches.

A regional edge cache helps to improve performance for a customer's viewers; it can be scaled to a customer's origin to reduce their origin costs. These caches are what sits between the edge locations and the CloudFront server. They have a larger cache-width than that of each edge locations cache.

To view the edge locations and regional edge caches around the world, you can go to the following AWS Link:

https://aws.amazon.com/cloudfront/features/?p=ugi&l=na

Architecture Design Principles of the Cloud

This section discusses the architecture for migrating to or deploying to the AWS Cloud and covers the basics to establish a well-architectured design solution.

AWS Well-Architected Framework

AWS provides the Well-Architect Framework in order to help customers become more aware of how their businesses are affected by their design decisions. The Well-Architect Framework has been designed by AWS experts to help ensure customers can assess and improve upon their design architecture.

By answering a few key questions developed by the AWS experts, customers can quickly assess if they are following best practices. These best practices are broken into 5 design perspectives known as the 5 Pillars, upon which the customer can measure the strength of their design.

The 5 Pillars are:

Security

This pillar is part of the design process that covers how the system is going to be designed to protect the customer's information. The system must be able to protect the customer's systems and data but still be able to deliver value by setting up various security strategies.

AWS Cloud security is made up of 5 areas which include:

- Identity and Access Management (IAM) — Controls the users and or systems that can access the customer's system to ensure only those granted access can gain access.

- Detection control tools — Systems that can identify any threats or potential threats to the system. These tools are set to efficiently scan, capture, and analyze logs in order to be able to identify a security or potential security threat.

- Infrastructure systems protection — With the use of firewalls, network boundaries, patching, user levels/access keys, and hardening the customer can protect their systems from potential security breaches.

- Data and information protection — Data protection can be applied by using data encryption, protecting data at rest and in transit, data backup, and data classification. Data protection also includes methods such as fall-back recovery and replications.

- Incident response process — Even though cloud security may seem it can run itself there are still potential risks. Incident response procedures should always be put into place and kept updated.

Security Design Principles
When designing the security pillar there are some design principles that should be taken into account and these principles include:

- Security must be implemented on all layers — In the AWS Cloud, customers can apply security at all levels and not just the perimeter level as is the procedure in most data centers.

- Traceability — Traceability gives the customer a clear few of any and all changes made throughout the system. This is done through various audits and logs that can be applied.

- Principle of least privilege should be applied — Keeping strong and strict access policies on the system and resources ensures only those that need access to certain areas, systems, or resources have access.

- The system needs to be the main focus for security — This is done by the AWS Shared Responsibility Model. AWS provides the secure infrastructure while the customer concentrates on securing their data and operating systems.

- Automate whenever or wherever possible — Automating security with software-based systems cuts down on risk and negligence from having to physically maintain the system. Automating is fast, can be set up on a timed basis, and ensures the system is always up to date.

Reliability

The reliability model encompasses the stability, resilience, and reliability of a system. In other words how quickly a system can recover from a failure, how reliable a system is, and how useful it is. Reliability is measured by how quickly the system can recover, how often it has downtime, and how efficiently it can meet the customer's demands.

The main fundamentals of the Reliability Pillar are:

- Ability to recover — A well-architected system must be resilient and have little to no downtime. It should also be able to recover with little to no data loss or deterioration of the system.

- Best practices to implement include

  - Failure management — A tried, tested, and up to data failure management plan should be implemented along with features that enable automatic healing of the system.

  - Change management — A valid change management plan needs to be implemented along with a solid outline and understanding of how certain system changes can affect business continuity.

  - Foundations — The foundation of the system should be built on taking into consideration the 5 pillars and all they entail.

- Ability to anticipate, respond, and prevent failures — A reliable system needs to be efficient enough to ensure that the customer can anticipate and respond to failure or change quickly and efficiently. It is also imperative to be able to prevent failures, whenever and wherever possible, by having resilient systems with failovers where necessary. With the cloud implementing new systems or stand-in, systems are more cost-efficient; this allows for the current system to be scrutinized for its problem areas.

Reliability Design Principles

When taking into account the reliability pillar there are some design principles that should be taken into account and these principles include:

- Recovery procedures should be tested on a regular basis

- Automated recovery procedures allow for the freeing up of critical resources to recover any downed systems.

- Replace large scale systems with smaller ones to prevent single points of failure and make the system more robust - this is known as scaling horizontally.

- Using a sliding scale to adapt to resource usage demand this will take the guesswork out of predicting what resources may be needed. By scaling capacity, it cuts down on cost and cuts out unused resources that are not cost-effective or are underutilized. This frees up capital to be used in places that need it more.

- Setting up any systems changed to be managed automatically. This cuts out having to manage small changes all over the system. Instead, you manage the automated change management system only.

Performance Efficiency

AWS offers many different solutions and it is up to the customer to choose the best solution for their requirements in order to get the best performance from the system.

Here are the basics that make up the Performance Efficiency Pillar:

- Customizable solutions are the best options — All AWS solutions are virtualized, this allows for customers to customize their solutions to better fit their needs.

- Continually review solutions to ensure constant innovation — New solutions come out all the time just like current ones are constantly updated and added to. Systems need to reviewed on a regular basis and adjusted, updated, or replaced as and when needed.

- AWS services should be monitored — Systems should be constantly monitored to ensure they are performing at their optimum, or are being under or over utilized. This can be automated with various threshold alarms set.

Performance Efficiency Design Principles

When taking into account the Performance Efficiency pillar there are some design principles that should be taken into account and these principles include:

- Advanced technology can be democratized whereby more complex systems can be taken care of by the vendor. For instance, complex systems do not need to be learned by current developers or IT staff. Instead, the vendors take care of the complex infrastructure freeing up the customer's developers and IT staff to concentrate on their work.

- Going global can be achieved as fast as pressing a button instead of having to have complex system rollouts.

- Serverless architecture frees up space, resources, and allows for the allocation of funds to be concentrated on other areas. It also ensures that the infrastructure is always up to date and has the capacity to suit the customer's requirements. It also means that the company does not need to employ technical IT experts to run the servers.

Cost Optimization

The Cost Optimization Pillar works on the basis that the customer can build and operate cost-efficient systems, while maximizing return on their investment. The four basic areas that make up the Cost Optimization pillar are:

- Utilize resources that are cost-effective

- Efficiently matching supply and demand

- Awareness of expenditure

- Over time, the system can easily be optimized further

Cost Optimization Design Principles
When taking into account the Cost Optimization Pillar, there are some design principles that should be taken into account and these principles include:

- By adopting a consumption model the customer only pays for resources that they are using or need.

- By measuring the overall efficiency of the system, the customer can judge how cost-effective the current system is and then adjust it accordingly.

- By fully utilizing the benefits, service, and features of the AWS Cloud, the customer can greatly reduce the costs of expensive data centers or on-premise based infrastructure.

- By using the AWS Managed services the customer has better control over their costs and billing processes.

Operational excellence

Operational excellence focuses on the running, monitoring, and maintenance of the AWS Cloud-based system to ensure the customer is getting operational excellence by delivering value. This is done by AWS's commitment to the continuous improvement of their systems, features, and solutions they have to offer their customers.

The four basic areas that make up the Operational Excellence pillar are:

- Changes are managed and automated

- Fast and efficient response to events

- Standards are defined and maintained as the system changes

Fault Tolerance Architecture

Fault tolerance is the system's ability to remain operational during times of various systems stresses. These stresses can include various components not working or software degeneration. It is the application's components built-in redundancy policy.

AWS Fault Tolerance Tools:
- Amazon Simple Queue Services (SQS)

    o Is the backbone of the fault tolerance service

- o   It is a distributed message service

- o   It is reliable and ensures the customer's queue is always available

- **Amazon Simple Storage Service (S3)**

  - o   Durable and fault-tolerant data storage solution

  - o   Simple web service that is always available

  - o   The customer only pays for storage used

  - o   Data is stored redundantly on multiple different devices. These devices can be distributed across multiple facilities in a region.

- **Amazon Relational Database Service (RDS)**

  - o   High availability and fault tolerance to enhance the reliability of a customer's critical databases.

  - o   Provides automated backup features

  - o   Snapshots

  - o   Deployment across multiple accessibility zones

High Availability Architecture

High availability of systems describes the reliability of the system where it is accessible and operational. This means that the system has to be available at set times or 24-hours as per the customer's requirements, with little to no downtime. High availability systems usually have a minimal human intervention with a cost-effective up-front financial outlay.

AWS High Availability Service Tools:

- Elastic load balancers (ELB)

    o Distributes load of incoming traffic

    o Updates Amazon CloudWatch with useful metrics

    o Notifies when certain thresholds are hit, these can be customized to suit the requirements of the customer.

        ▪ Over utilization

        ▪ High latency

- Elastic IP addresses

    o Static IP addresses designed for dynamic cloud computing

- They allow uses to use the same IP address with different resources

- Static IP addresses ensure high availability as resources can still be accessed during an instance failure

- Amazon Route 53

  - Authoritative DNS Service used to translate domain names to IP addresses

  - Route 53 supports; latency-based routing, health checks, DNS failovers, Geo-locations routing, and Simple routing.

- Auto Scaling

  - Is used to create new, on-demand resources

  - Is used to assist with modifying or adjusting system capacity

  - Can both launch or terminate instances

- Amazon CloudWatch

  - CloudWatch is a system that is used for distributed statistics gathering

- It is used to track customers' infrastructure metrics

- It is customizable so that customers can also track their own set metrics

- CloudWatch works hand-in-hand with Auto Scaling

AWS Solution for Fault Tolerance and High Availability

AWS offers systems that are fault-tolerant and offer high availability. AWS solutions are customizable and offer services that span multiple servers across multiple availability zones, and even regions if necessary.

Test Your Knowledge

When you have completed this chapter, which is the Domain 1 - Cloud Concepts domain of the CCP course you should be able to:

- Define cloud computing

- Define how the cloud works

- Describe the advantages, benefits, and discuss the AWS Cloud value proposition

- Have a basic understanding of the global cloud infrastructure

- Define the differences between regions, availability zones, and edge locations.

- Define the different cloud deployment methods

- Define the basic AWS Cloud architectural principles

- Define the Well-Architected Framework

- Describe fault tolerance architecture

- Describe high availability architecture

Test Questions

Here are a few practice sample exam questions to help test your knowledge; please see the section under **Chapter 8** for the answers to **Chapter 2: Cloud Concepts Test Questions Answers.**

Question 1: Choose the term that best describes the ability to upscale or downscale resources:

Choose 1 out of 4

1. Efficiency

2. Expediency

3. Effortless

4. Elastic

Question 2: Which of the following forms part of the 5 Pillars of AWS Well-Architected Framework?

Choose 3 out of 5

1. Reliability

2. Elastic

3. Cost Optimization

4. Security

5. Persistence

.

Chapter 3

Security

Customers can run a wide range of applications that are offered with AWS Cloud solutions. These solutions run on a highly available and dependable cloud computing platform that is completely scalable to suit customer needs.

As more and more individuals, small to medium, and even large corporations move to cloud-based computing systems, cloud hosting companies have to offer high levels of security. AWS is always striving to ensure its security measures are in place and highly effective to protect customers' systems and information.

As AWS needs to stay ahead of its competitor's security is of the utmost importance. That is why they offer properly secured solutions that are fully compliant and in some cases can offer more advanced security than that of some hybrid or on-premise solutions.

AWS is continually improving upon their security services that were created by experts to offer customers advanced security service. The customer needs are met at lower operating costs as they only pay for the security features they use. Any issues that arise are addressed in real-time, creating a fully compliant and secure environment.

Cloud-based, governance-enabled security features mean the customer has greater security oversight, and control along with central automation.

Security Support Resources

AWS provides tools for monitoring and logging giving the customer full visibility into their environment. There are several tools and features offered by AWS that increase the customers' security and services to ensure their data is secure and there are no privacy violations while controlling network access.

Some of these features include

- Built-in firewalls

- Encryption in transit

- Private connections

- Distributed denial of service (DDoS) mitigation

    o   AWS Shield is a managed service of DDos

AWS offers inventory and configuration management tools to help manage security which include:

- Deployment tools

- Inventory and configuration tools

- Template definition tools

- Management tools

AWS offers data encryption features for data at rest in the cloud, which include:

- Encryption capabilities

  o Amazon EBS

  o Amazon S3

  o Amazon Glacier

  o Oracle RDS

  o SQL Server RDS

  o Amazon Redshift

- Key management options

  o AWS Key Management Service (KMS)

- Hardware-based cryptographic key storage options

  o AWS CloudHSM

AWS Access Control and Management Features

- Identity and Access Management (IAM)

  o Create user accounts across AWS system

  o Assign user account permission

- Multi-factor authentication (MFA)

  o Use with privileged accounts

  o Hardware-based authentication

- Integration and federation with corporate directories

  o Reduces administration costs

  o Improves user experiences

AWS Monitoring and Logging Features

AWS offers many monitoring and logging tools and features that help to reduce the customer's risk profile. Features include:

- Alert notifications

- Log aggregation and options

- Deep visibility into calls to APIs

AWS Shared Responsibility Model

When a customer joins AWS Cloud, security becomes a shared responsibility. In other words both the customer and AWS are responsible for the security and compliance of systems, data, and applications being used in the cloud.

The AWS Shared Responsibility Model defines that AWS is responsible for:

- The security of the cloud

    o AWS is responsible for the security of the infrastructure upon which the cloud runs.

    o This infrastructure includes:

        ➢ Hardware

        ➢ Software

        ➢ Networking

        ➢ AWS Cloud services facilities

The AWS Shared Responsibility Model defines that the AWS customer is responsible for:

- The security within the cloud

    o IAM user access management

o IAM user access controls

o Data encryption - client and server-side

o Operating system patches

o Operating and software updates

o EC2 includes security groups and network-level security

Test Your Knowledge

When you have completed this chapter, which is the Domain 2 - Security domain of the CCP course, you should be able to:

- Define the AWS Cloud security services

- Have a clear understanding of shared security

- Define the Shared Responsibility Model

Here are a few practice sample exam questions to help test your knowledge; please see the section under **Chapter 8** for the answers to **Chapter 3: Security Test Questions Answers**.

Question 1: Which statement is true for the Shared Responsibility Model?

Choose 1 out of 4

1. AWS is responsible for the security of the infrastructure upon which the cloud runs.

2. The customer is responsible for the security of the infrastructure upon which the cloud runs.

3. AWS is responsible for security within the cloud.

4. AWS is not responsible for any security within the customer's cloud infrastructure.

Chapter 4

Technology

This chapter covers the AWS organization and accounts as well as Amazon core services that makeup AWS technology services.

AWS Organization and Accounts

As with any system when you first sign up you have to create an account. AWS has four different types of account levels.

Organization

The Organization is the company or customer and allows for centralized billing management, resource sharing, access control, security control, compliance, and AWS membership accounts control.

Root User Account

When you first start using AWS you have to create a user account, this user account becomes the Root Account User. It is a single account and is like the administrator account on an MS Windows system. The Root user has access to all the customer's AWS services, resources, and information. Every user account will have a Root user.

Organization Units

These are organizational units that can be created to split and group AWS accounts for the quick access and control of common shared resources and applications. Organization units can also contain other organization units to create a hierarchical structure.

Service Control Policies

These are policies that help to group various access controls giving central control over various permissions for all a customer's accounts. Service control policies allow for uniformed permissions across resources and ensure all policies are compliant with that of the organization's policies and guidelines.

AWS Networking

When the customer first starts using AWS they have to choose the region to launch their system in as well as the AZ which is the data center that houses the AWS resources. Different AZs can offer different resources. Not all AZs have all the AWS resources so a customer has chosen the region and AZ based on their resource requirements.

Amazon Virtual Private Cloud (VPC)

After a region and AZ have been established the customer will need a VPC. The VPC is where the customer will launch their

AWS resources. It is their logically isolated portion of the cloud that gets assigned for their use.

Internet Gateway

Next the internet gateway will be enabled which grants the customer access to the internet along with setting up of the routing tables and network ACL **(NACL).** A subnet partitions a logical IP network into smaller portions or segments; like a housing development built on one property. Instead of one large house on 54 Main street, there are now ten houses and their addresses become a subdivision of the main address.

Security Groups

A security group on AWS is a type of firewall positioned at the instance level of the cloud.

AWS Core Services

AWS comes with a host of core and integrated services to ensure customers get the services they need. These services can be broken into the following:

Database Services

There are a number of AWS database services and some of the most widely used ones are:

AWS Relational Database Service (RDS)

RDS is the most widely used of the database services on AWS because it supports multiple database engines. These database engines include:

- MySQL

- Maria DB

- Oracle

- Aurora

- Microsoft SQL

- Postgres

Aurora

Aurora is a fully managed database that can run PSQL 3 x faster and MySQL 5 x faster than legacy systems cans. Aurora is a lot more expensive than most other database services.

Aurora Serverless

Aurora Serverless is a database that is much like AWS Lambda and only runs when the customer needs it to. This makes Aurora serverless a lot less expensive than Aurora.

DocumentDB

The DocumentDB database is compatible with MongoDB and is a NoSQL document database.

DymamoDB

It is a database that is based on Cassandra. It is a NoSQL key/value database. It will guarantee many reads or write per second.

ElastiCache

ElastiCache database is a caching source that is compatible with databases such as open-source Memcached and Redis.

Neptune

The only thing students need to know about Neptune is that it is a managed graph database.

Redshift

The main information students need to know about Redshift is that it is a columnar store database that can run a warehouse-type application that requires petabytes of information. For all those that do not know 1 petabyte (PB) is 1000 TB.

Provisioning Services

AWS uses various services to automate the setting up of a customer's services, resources, or systems.

There are a few AWS Core Services that are used for provisioning and these include:

AWS QuickStart

AWS Quickstart is a service that contains automated packages to help with the deployment of a workload on AWS. It is there to help with the configuration of AWS services such as the network, storage, and AWS compute.

AWS Marketplace

AWS Marketplace is, as the name suggests, an AWS marketplace where a customer can find a multitude of vendors, to buy various software, platforms for testing apps, and deploying software. It is also the place to go in order to sell or bid on unused AWS instances.

CloudFormation

This works for infrastructure as code and creates a template using either YAML or JSON file.

Elastic Beanstalk

Is a simple service used for scaling as well as deploying web applications. Elastic Beanstalk is compatible with applications created in .NET, PHP, Node.js, Python, Ruby, Docker, Java, and Go. It is a simple application for uploading code that needs little to no tweaking to work.

OpsWorks

OpsWorks provides Puppet and Chef to help with configuration management services.

AWS Computing

AWS computing core services include the following:

Amazon Elastic Cloud Compute (EC2)

Amazon EC2 is a web service with the following features:

- Provides complete control

- Allows the configuration of capacity

- Provides resizable compute capacity

Everything on AWS runs on EC2 instances as it is an Elastic Compute cloud that allows for the full configuration of the operating system, network, memory, and CPU in the cloud environment.

Elastic Container Service (ECS)

This service is highly scalable and provides Docker as a service. This provides high-performance orchestration of containers that supports Docker containers. The customer will have to pay for the EC2 to run this service.

EKS

EKS is a service that is easy to manage, scale containerized applications using Kubernetes. It is Kubernetes as a service that is really easy to deploy.

Elastic Beanstalk

Elastic Beanstalk is the service that operates the various AWS services. These services include Simple Notification Services (SNS), EC2 Amazon S3, CloudWatch, Elastic Load Balancers, auto scaling, and CloudWatch.

Lambda

Lambda is a service that you only pay for when it is in use. It is a serverless service that is used to deploy or run code on without having to manage, invest in, or configure servers.

AWS Storage Services

Amazon Elastic Block Store (EBS)

Amazon EBS is used with Amazon EC2 instances to provide block-level storage volumes. EBS volumes exist independent from an instance as they are off-instance storage volumes.

They are the virtual disk of the AWS cloud for which there are three types of EBS volumes:

- General Purpose (SSD)

- Magnetic

- Provisional IOPS (SSD)

Amazon Simple Storage Service (S3)

Amazon S3 is an internet or cloud storage space much like DropBox or GoogleDrive. Only S3 can be used to store any size of data that can be accessed from anywhere over the web at any time.

Amazon S3 features include:
- Object storage

- Can store any amount of data

- Can be used to retrieve data from anywhere at any time

- S3 is durable

- S3 is scalable

- Uses query in place

- S3 has flexible data management

- Has flexible data transfer capabilities

- S3 is compatible and supported by AWS services as well as AWS partners, and various vendors

Elastic File Storage (EFS)

This storage solution can be mounted to two or more EC2 instances at the same time.

S3 Glacier

S3 Glacier is a simple low-cost solution that is not ideal for instances where you need fast access to data. It is more for the use of long-term backup and archiving solutions. Anyone who has ever gone to either backup or restores data will understand how S3 Glacier works as accessing files takes a long time.

Snowball

Snowball uses computer suitcase-type technology to move large amounts of data.

Storage Gateway

Storage Gateway bridges the gap for use with hybrid cloud solutions using local caching.

AWS Logging Services

AWS has a few services that help customers with system audit trails in order to keep a close watch on changes to the AWS system, as well as when those changes were made and by whom.

CloudTrail

CloudTrail audits and logs all calls that were made to APIs from AWS services. This service helps to determine pieces of information such as:

- AWS EC2 instance usage

- Who launched certain applications and when

- Who created a bucket

CloudTrail helps the customer to:

- Determine any misconfiguration that may have been made by a developer or administrator

- Create automated responses

- Help detect and deal with any malicious actors within the system

CloudWatch

CloudWatch is made up of a host of different services that are used for logging information such as performance, various system metrics and events. It is used to speed up delivery for customers of their content across the globe. Some of these services include:

- CloudWatch Alarms

  - Set threshold alarms, failure alarms, various alerts, etc.

  - Set notifications for various metrics

- CloudWatch Dashboard

  - Metrics-based dashboard that can be customized to visualize various logs, metrics, etc.

- CloudWatch Events

  - Service that will trigger an alarm for set thresholds

  - Based on certain triggers the system could take a backup snapshot

  - Set an event to happen every day, hour, week, etc.

- CloudWatch Logs

  - This CloudWatch service logs CPU Utilization, Memory performance and utilization, Lambda logs, Rails, Nginx, and so on.

  - Keep the threshold or even logs.

- CloudWatch Metrics

  - Creates and monitors various metrics based on time-ordered data points.

  - Variable monitor

AWS Initialisms

As with most information technology services, there are multiple initialisms. It is good to know what they are to help you quickly navigate the exam and stop from being tripped up on trick questions.

- ALB — Application Load Balancer

- ASG — Auto Scaling Group

- BI — Business Intelligence

- CFN — CloudFormation

- EB — Elastic Beanstalk

- EBS — Elastic Block Storage

- EC2 — Elastic Cloud Compute

- ECS — Elastic Container Service

- ECR — Elastic Container Repository

- EFS — Elastic Fiber Storage

- EKS — Elastic Kubernetes Service

- EMR — Elastic MapReduce

- ES — Elasticsearch

- IAM — Identity and Access Management

- IMAP — Internet Message Access Protocol

- IoT — Internet of Things

- MKS — Managed Kafka Service

- MQ — Amazon ActiveMQ

- NLB — Network Load Balancer

- RDS — Relational Database Service

- RI — Reserved Instances

- S3 — Simple Storage Services

- SES — Simple Email Services

- SQS — Simple Queue Service

- SSM — Simple Systems Manager

- SWF — Simple Workflow Service

- TAM — Technical Account Manager

- VPC — Virtual Private Cloud

- VPN — Virtual Private Network

- WAF — Web Application Firewall

AWS Business Services

AWS offers a host of business-centric services designed to help businesses meet various business requirements, like that of service centers, remote working clients, etc.

Some of these services include the more widely used ones such as:

- **Amazon Connect** — Call center service

  - This is easy to set up and use a call center service system that is a version of the Amazon customer service system.

- **Chime** — Online video conferencing, meetings, and calling system.

  - Chime is a platform designed for businesses to have online meetings and conferences, training sessions, and calls.

- o Chime is elastically scalable to meet business needs, as it can be scaled to offer more or less capacity as and when required by the customer.

- **Pinpoint** — Marketing campaign management service

  - o Pinpoint is used for email marketing campaigns.

  - o Pinpoint can be used for SMS, voice message notifications, and push notification for target marketing.

- **QuickSight** — Business intelligence service

  - o Business metrics from multiple databases at one time.

  - o Takes hardly any programming skills to set up or use.

  - o Allows for data to visualize in the form of graphs.

- **SES** — Simple Email Service

  - o Simple email service that can be used to send out marketing information, emails, and notifications.

  - o Mainly designed for marketers and developers.

- **WorkDocs** — Collaboration and content creation workspace in AWS

    ○ Similar to SharePoint where a customer can share, edit, and create content that is saved in AWS across their business system hosted on AWS.

- **WorkMail** — AWS work-based email system

    ○ Store, create, and send emails.

    ○ Store email addresses, contacts, and calendar.

    ○ Supports most (IMAP) mobile client applications.

    ○ Supports most (IMAP) desktop client applications.

- **WorkSpaces** — Virtual Remote Desktop service

    ○ The customer can provision hundreds of either Windows or Linux desktops.

Test Your Knowledge

When you have completed this chapter, which is the Domain 3 - Technology domain of the CCP course, you should be able to:

- Define the different AWS Core Services

- Define the different AWS Integrated Services

- Describe the technology support resources

Test Question

Here is a practice sample exam question to help test your knowledge; please see the section under **Chapter 8** for the answer to **Chapter 4: Technology Test Question Answers**.

Question 1: Which of the following are AWS Database services?

Choose 2 out of 5

1. ElastiCache

2. CloudFormation

3. Elastic Container Service (ECS)

4. RDS

5. Elastic File Storage (EFS)

Chapter 5

Billing and Pricing

AWS billing and pricing philosophy states that the customer only pays for the services they have used in a pay-as-you-go billing scenario. These services do not tie a customer into a contract and the customer gets to use the services they have requested for as long as they need them.

Although AWS offers a host of different features and services available to the customer, the customer only pays for the exact amount of usage for each one. At the end of each month the customer only pays for what they actually used during the month and there are no long-term contracts.

AWS allows the customer to:

- Pay as you go

- Pay less when they reserved services

- The more of a service they use the less they pay for it

- As AWS grows, their services get even cheaper

- EC2 is the only instance that needs to have a reserved capacity

- AWS has no termination fees; when you no longer need a service, you stop using it and paying for it

- There is a free tier service that allows customers to run certain services for free

  - free tier includes offers that expire after 12 months

  - free tier includes some offers that never expire

AWS Pricing Models

AWS pricing models policies include:

- Custom pricing for enterprise customers

- Pay as you go

- Pay less when you reserved

- Pay even less per unit the more you use the service

- Pay even less the bigger AWS customer base grows

AWS has free services which include:

- *OpsWorks*

- Consolidated Billing

- Amazon VPC

- CloudFormation (does not include created resources)

- Identity Access Management (IAM)

- Auto Scaling (does not include created resources)

- Elastic Beanstalk (does not include created resources)

- Inbound data transfer

- 1 Free Elastic IP address

- Data transfer between regions

AWS the customer pays for:

- *Compute capacity*

- Storage

- Outbound data transfer

AWS Pricing for AWS Core Services

Amazon EC2

- *AWS only charges for the capacity the customer has used.*

- AWS EC2 instances prices include the operating system.

- Some vendors are partnered with AWS to help with licensing so that the customer can bring their licenses with them.

- Most other software packages will need vendor licenses.

- Cost factors for EC2

  - **On-demand** instances require the least commitment from the customer

    - Has a minimum usage of 60 seconds

    - Compute capacity is charged for usage by the hour and second

    - Flexible

    - This is a great option for a workload that needs to run uninterrupted

    - This is a great option for short-term, unpredictable workloads, and new apps

  - **Reserved** instances are great for getting large discounts and is the best option for long-term usage options

- This is a great option for predictable as well as steady-state usage

- Reserved instances that are not used can be sold on the AWS marketplace

- Reserved instances get a discounted hour rate

- Payment terms are usually 1 or 3 years

- There are 3 class offerings:

    - Convertible

    - Scheduled

    - Standard

- Payment options are: upfront, no upfront, or partial upfront

- Reservations apply to the following services:

    - Amazon DynamoDB Reserved Capacity

    - Amazon ElatiCache Reserved Nodes

- Amazon RDS Reserved Instances

- Amazon RedShift Reserved Instances

o **Spot** instances allow for up to 90% discounts, which offer the biggest savings

- Here a customer gets to bid on the capacity that is unused

- Start and end times are flexible

- AWS can, at any time, terminate the instances

- If AWS terminates the instance, the customer is not charged

- If the customer terminates the instance, they are still charged

o **Dedicated Hosting** which is the most expensive

- There are dedicated services

- Can use on-demand or reserved

Amazon s3

When the customer is looking at S3 they need to consider the following storage classes:

- Standard storage

  - 99.99999999% durable

  - 99.99% availability

- Standard-Infrequent Access

  - 99.99999999% durable

  - 99.99% availability

- Storage Cost

  - Number of objects

  - Size of objects

  - Type of Storage

- Amazon S3 all have different rates depending on:

  - Storage: The number and size of the object stored in the S3 buckets and the type of storage

- o Requests: The number and type of requests for instance:

  - ■ Get requests to have different costs to that of PUT and COPY requests

- o Data transfer: The amount of data transferred out of the Amazon S3 environment

Amazon EBS

Each of the EBS volumes types differ in performance and cost, offering the customer a choice that better suits their application needs. For EBS costing the following needs to be taken into consideration:

- Volumes: Each type of volume is provisioned per month upon which the cost will be based

- Input Output will vary depending on the volume type:

  - o General Purpose (SSD) is included in the price

  - o Magnetic gets charged per request

  - o Provisioned IOPS (SSD) is provisioned by the customer

- A snapshot enables a snapshot for data backup and is charged per gigabyte of data stored

- Data transfer minuses the inbound data transfer (which is for free) and charges a tiered rate for outbound data transfer

AWS Support Plans

AWS goes to great lengths to provide customers with the correct services and resources. It also strives to ensure there is a plan that will suit the needs, requirements, and pricing for everyone.

AWS support plans have been developed to ensure they help meet the customer's needs and are right there at their fingertips. This includes even the customers taking AWS for a test drive. Because AWS support covers a diverse spectrum of customers from the test-driving customer, customers using AWS for production use, to those that use AWS for business critical application, there are different support plans.

AWS has three different kinds of support which are:

- **Account assistance**
  - An AWS Support Concierge helps the customer with account assistance.

  - The support concierge is an AWS billing and pricing expert.

  - They will attend to all non-technical calls that refer to various billing, pricing, and account-level inquiries.

- **Best practices support**
  - *A Trusted Advisor is assigned to the customer.*

  - Trusted advisors are the resident AWS Cloud expert.

  - The Trusted Advisor will continuously monitor the cloud for better solutions and optimize the cloud to ensure the customer never misses opportunities that will benefit them.

  - The Trusted Advisor will also continuously monitor and help the customer do cost optimization and increase productivity.

- **Proactive guidance support**
  - Technical Account Manager (TAM) is assigned to the customer.

  - The TAM provides the customer with assistance and guidance in:

    - Architectural review of the system

    - Help with preparing and planning deployment of AWS

- Help with optimizing current solutions or planned ones

- They are the customer's advisor for AWS

Currently, AWS has four different plans that are available, and these are:

You can find the AWS most up-to-date support plans on their website or by following the link below:

https://aws.amazon.com/premiumsupport/pricing/

- **Basic** – Access to only the billing, account support only and access only to the AWS forums. This is the plan you get when you first create an AWS account.

- **Business** — Access to 24/7 chat, phone, and email support. Unlimited users can open unlimited cases.

- **Developer** – This is business hours support that can be accessed through email. One person can open unlimited cases.

- **Enterprise** – Access to 24/7 chat, phone and email support. Unlimited users can open unlimited cases. A Technical Account Manager (TAM) comes with this support option.

Consolidated Billing

Consolidated billing is one bill that incorporates multiple AWS accounts. This is really handy when a customer has multiple accounts or payment methods. It also comes at no extra cost and the customer can use Cost Explorer to get a real-time view of their usage.

With consolidated billing, there is one master account that gets set up to manage all the member accounts for the customer.

Volume Discounts

A major benefit of consolidated billing is the volume discount that gets assigned to the customer. As you now know, the more you use AWS services, the cheaper the usage price. As the customer is consolidating all their membership services into one bill, it is seen as one member using all those services.

AWS Cost Explorer

AWS Cost Explorer is a way for customers to visualize their usage, as well as manage and understand these costs.

AWS Cost Explorer comes with a host of useful reports that help the customer gain valuable insight into usage trends and cost drivers for their organization's account. There are predesigned reports and reports that the customer can design themselves.

Cost Explorer also offers a forecasting feature to the customer to predict future AWS costs.

AWS Budgets

AWS Budgets is a tool that can help the customer to plan their service costs, instance reservations, and service usage. They can set threshold alarms, print out reports, and do forecasting. The first few budgets are free; after that there is a small charge per budget created.

AWS Trusted Advisor

AWS Trusted Advisor is a service that helps customers keep track of the services and make sure they are observing best practices. The service does this by continuously observing the customer AWS environment. It is designed to make sure the system is cost-effective in order to keep saving the customer money. It will ensure that the systems are running at top performance, that they are reliable, and it will close any gaps in the system's security.

It runs as a dashboard service whereby the customer can observe their AWS systems:

- Cost Optimization stats

- Performance

- Security

- Fault tolerance

- Service limits

- Set preferences

In a nutshell, AWS Trusted Advisor is a service or tool the customer can use to find real-time guidance to help them better provision their resources and ensure they are following AWS best practices.

Test Your Knowledge

When you have completed this chapter, which is the Domain 4 - Billing and Pricing domain of the CCP course, you should be able to:

- Define AWS Billing for the AWS platform

- Define pricing modules for the AWS platform

- Understand account management for the AWS platform

- Discuss sources of documentation

- Discuss technical assistance

Test Questions

Here are a few practice sample exam questions to help test your knowledge; please see the section under **Chapter 8** for the answers to **Chapter 5: Billing and Pricing Test Questions Answers**.

Question 1: Which of the following is not an AWS free service?

Choose 2 out of 5

1. Consolidated Billing

2. Compute capacity

3. Amazon VPC

4. Data transfer between regions

5. Outbound data transfer

Question 2: From the following statements, choose the option that best describes AWS Trusted advisor:

Choose 1 out of 4

1. A service or tool that helps customers analyze their usage.

2. A service or tool that provides the customer with real-time guidance to help them provision their resources to ensure they follow AWS best practices.

3. A service or tool that helps customers analyze their monthly AWS costs.

4. A service or tool that provides the customer with a visual of their total monthly AWS billing.

Chapter 6

The Exam

When you go to take the exam, you will do so through a computer-simulated test which can be taken at an exam center, as an online proctored exam, or at an exam center. This chapter explains what to expect of the test, what a proctored exam is, what to expect from the testing center, and testing centers where the exam can be taken.

What to Expect From the Exam
The exam consists of 65 questions that you will need to complete in 90-minutes.

hese questions consist of:

Multiple-Choice Questions
- Multiple-choice questions you will need to choose one answer from a possible four answers.

Multiple-Response Questions

These questions will have 5 or more answers of which you will be asked to choose 2 or more answers. The question will let you know how many answers you need to choose, for example:

Choose 2 out 5

White Papers to Read for the Course and Exam

- Overview of Amazon Web Services

- How AWS Pricing Works

- Architecting for the Cloud: AWS Best Practices

- Cost Management in the AWS Cloud

Proctored Exam

Some AWS certifications, which included the AWS CCP certification, offer proctored exams. These are exams that a person can take in the comfort of their own homes or their place of work.

Requirements for a Proctored Exam:

- A computer that has a webcam, audio, and at least 1 GB of free disk space.

- The computer must be compatible with, and able to download the proctoring software the exam institute will provide the test taker.

- You must have a form ID to verify who you are and the ability to be able to take your picture with your ID before, after, and if necessary during the exam.

- A good, stable internet connection that is capable of being able to handle the monitoring software.

- The exam-taker must be aware of and fully understand the exam rules of both the course provider and proctoring software.

How Proctored Exams Work:

If a course offers the option for a proctored exam, they will have certain rules which the student will be given upon registering for the proctored exam. The student will be given the proctored exam software access, which they will have to download onto their computer or device upon which they will take the exam.

It is up to the student to ensure that the system they are taking the exam on is compatible with the exam format and that they have a stable internet connection.

The student will register, and show their ID credentials. During the exam, the proctoring software will monitor the student's computer desktop, the audio, and video through the webcam.

Once you have completed the exam, the exam session will be reviewed by the proctoring service; results are usually sent back to the student within 5 working days after exam submission.

It is very important to ensure you fully understand and follow the rules of a proctored exam.

Exam Centers that Offer the CCP Exam

You can also book the exam through the AWS website for your convenience at the following website address:

https://www.aws.training/Certification

All you have to do is create an AWS Certification account.

Pearson VUE

Pearson VUE is the main testing center for most Information Technology or related exams. You can do the AWS certifications through this testing facility. They also have very good exam simulations to help you get ready for the actual certification exam.

You can access the website for AWS exams from the following link:

https://home.pearsonvue.com/aws/contact

What you Need to Know About Test Centers

There Pearson VUE tests centers situated throughout the United States of America and globally. There are also affiliated test centers should there not be one near to you. You can check them by going to the Pearson VUE website at the following link:

https://home.pearsonvue.com/Test-takers.aspx

Pearson VUE usually has more than one test centers in major cities. Students are allowed to switch between them in order to find the perfect exam time appointment. The websites are full of helpful information about taking the exam, the test centers, and the exam itself.

Before the test the student should:

- Be confident they are ready to take the exam.

- Find a test center near them.

- Check for available time slots.

- Make sure to register and pay for the exam at the time of booking the exam.

- Make sure they have all the necessary information, rules, and regulations for taking the exam.

- If a student is unable to take the exam on the scheduled day, they need to give at least 24-hours notice; or have valid documentation to back up their reason for not attending, if they cannot give 24-hours notice.

- If the student is unable to take the exam on the scheduled day, re-booking the exam is their responsibility.

- The student should check if there are penalties for not being able to take the exam on a registered day.

On exam day:

- The student should be well-rested and have a good meal before the exam.

- The student should arrive at the test center at least 30-minutes prior to the exam.

- The student needs to have proper identification with them.

- The student will not be allowed to take any mobile device, stationary, or anything with them into the exam.

- The student is usually issued a locker where they will have to put anything they may take to the institutions with them.

- The student will be provided with stationery for use during the exam by the staff of the exam center.

- The exam is held in a room where there will usually be a camera that monitors the room.

- There will be a computer in which the exam institute will issue the student with a password word to log in in with.

- The student, if they do not already have one, will be assigned a student number.

- The student must read every question and make sure they have understood it and answered to their best knowledge.

- When the exam is done, the results will usually be displayed on the screen immediately.

- The exam results are also printed out in the exam institutes office; you will be provided a copy of when you leave.

- You can take the exam again, should you need to, usually within 5 days.

- Your certification will be mailed to your registered residential address.

Chapter 7

AWS Certified Cloud Practitioner Test Questions

There are 65 questions when taking the CCP exam, for which you have 90 minutes to complete. There are a few places where you can get simulated exams to test your knowledge, these institutes may charge for the simulation.

Test simulators for the CCP exam can be found at:

- AWS — https://www.aws.training/certification

- Pearsons VUE - https://home.pearsonvue.com/aws/onvue

Here are 20 practice sample exam questions to help test your knowledge; please see the section under chapter 8 for the answers.

Questions

Question 1: Of the following services, which have Distributed Denial of Service (DDOS) mitigation features?

Choose 2 out of 5

1. Amazon CloudFront

2. AWS WAF

3. Amazon Inspector

4. Amazon EC2

5. Amazon DynamoDB

Question 2: To launch a new Amazon Relational Database Service (AWS RDS) cluster, what services would the customer need?

Choose 2 out of 5

1. Amazon EC2 Auto Scaling

2. AWS CloudFormation

3. AWS Concierge

4. Amazon S3

5. AWS Management Console

Question 3: AWS compliance reports needs which of the following services to provide on-demand access?

Choose 1 out of 4

1. AWS KMS

2. Amazon GuardDuty

3. AWS Artifact

4. AWS Concierge

Question 4: Which of the options below choose the AWS service that offers a fully managed NoSQL database service?

Choose 1 out of 4

1. Elastic Map Reduce

2. AWS RDS

3. Oracle RDS

4. DynamoDB

Question 5: What is the legacy application model called that web servers running on Amazon EC2 need to access?

Choose 1 out of 4

1. Infrastructure as a service (IaaS)

2. Software as a service (SaaS)

3. Partner Network

4. Hybrid architecture

Question 6: What are the factors that could influence a customer's decision when deciding upon an AWS Region for deploying a new application.

Choose 2 out of 6
1. Address regulatory compliance

2. Reduce latency

3. If the application is in the local language

4. Proximity to the customer's offices

5. Minimize costs

6. Data center cooling costs in hotter climates

Question 7: For static websites which is the best AWS service?

Choose 1 out of 4
1. AWS X-Ray

2. Amazon S3

3. Amazon Route 53

4. Infrastructure as a Service (IaaS)

Question 8: From the following options which answers describe the characteristics of Amazon S3?

Choose 3 out of 5

1. A single object can be up to 5 TB in size

2. A relational database is needed to be hosted by S3

3. Data is stored in resources called buckets as objects

4. S3 allows for the storing of virtually unlimited sized objects

5. Objects are accessible via a URL

Question 9: An organization has a requirement to move 12 TB of data to the AWS cloud. Which of the following Amazon services would be suitable to move such large amounts of data to the AWS cloud?

Choose 1 out of 4

1. Amazon Snowball

2. Amazon S3 Multipart Upload

3. Amazon Direct Connect

4. Amazon S3 Connector

Question 10: If a customer suspects an AWS account has been compromised, what should the customer do?

Choose 3 out of 6

1. Remove MFA tokens

2. Choose a different AWS region to move their resources to

3. Contact AWS support

4. Rotate access keys

5. Remove the AWS CloudTrail Resources

6. Rotate passwords

Question 11: What are the costs included with AWS on-premises total cost of ownership (TOC)?

Choose 1 out of 4

1. Infrastructure Management

2. Project Management

3. Business Analysis

4. Data Center Security

Question 12: Choose the AWS managed Domain Name System (DNS) web service from the following:

Choose 1 out of 4

1. Amazon S3

2. Amazon SageMaker

3. Amazon Route 53

4. Amazon Neptune

Question 13: For uninterruptible workloads that run for 24 hours once a year, which is the most cost-effective Amazon EC2 pricing model?

Choose 1 out of 4

1. Spot instances

2. Dedicated instances

3. On-demand instances

4. Reserved instances

Question 14: To ensure the lowest possible latency for large amounts of online video content, which are the two best AWS services to use?

Choose 2 out of 5

1. Amazon CloudFront

2. EFS

3. AWS Storage Gateway

4. Amazon S3

5. Amazon Route 53

Question 15: Choose the AWS Well-Architected Framework design principle that is related to reliability from the following options:

Choose 1 out of 4

1. The ability to recover from failure

2. Single availability zone deployment

3. Perform operations as code

4. A framework design principle that is optimized for cost

Question 16: Of the AWS Global Infrastructure components, which components consist of one or more discrete data centers interconnected through low latency links?

Choose 1 out of 4

1. Edge locations

2. Private networking

3. Region

4. Availability zone

Question 17: From the following features choose the AWS IAM feature that allows for access of AWS services through the AWS CLI for developers:

Choose 1 out of 4

1. Access keys

2. Passwords

3. SSH keys

4. Usernames

Question 18: AWS Cloud's multiple regions are an example of:

Choose 1 out of 4

1. Elasticity

2. On-demand services

3. Global infrastructure

4. Agility

Question 19: When hosting static websites, which is a low-cost storage service option?

Choose 1 out of 4

1. Amazon DynamoDB

2. Amazon S3

3. Amazon Route 53

4. Amazon EFS

Question 20: Which of the following AWS billing options ensures the reduction of costs for a customer who has multiple accounts?

Choose 1 out of 4

1. Consolidated billing

2. Multiple accounts are going to be costly and cannot be reduced

3. AWS automatically discounts multiple accounts

4. Combined billing

Chapter 8

Test Question Answers

Answers are listed per chapter from Chapter 2 through to Chapter 7 (excluding Chapter 6).

Chapter 2: Cloud Concepts Test Question Answers
Question 1:

    4. Elastic

Question 2:

    1. Reliability

    3. Cost Optimization

    4. Security

Chapter 3: Security Test Question Answers
Question 1:

    1. AWS is responsible for the security of the infrastructure upon which the cloud runs.

Chapter 4: Technology Test Question Answers

Question 1:

1. ElastiCache

4. RDS

Chapter 5: Billing and Pricing Test Question Answers

Question 1:

2. Compute Capacity

5. Outbound data transfer

Question 2:

2. A service or tool that provides the customer with real-time guidance to help them provision their resources to ensure they follow AWS best practices.

Chapter 7: AWS Certified Cloud Practitioner Test Questions Answers

Question 1:

6. Amazon CloudFront

7. AWS WAF

Question 2:

8. AWS Concierge

5. AWS Management Console

Question 3:

   3. AWS Artifact

Question 4:

   4. DynamoDB

Question 5:

   4. Hybrid architecture

Question 6:

   1. Address regulatory compliance

   2. Reduce latency

   5. Minimize costs

Question 7:

   2. Amazon S3

Question 8:

   1. A single object can be up to 5 TB in size

   3. Data is stored in resources called buckets as objects

   5. Objects are accessible via a URL

Question 9:

   1. Amazon Snowball

Question 10:

    3. Contact AWS support

    4. Rotate access keys

    6. Rotate passwords

Question 11:

    4. Data Center security

Question 12:

    3. Amazon Route 53

Question 13:

    3. On-demand instances

Question 14:

    1. Amazon CloudFront

    4. Amazon S3

Question 15:

    1. The ability to recover from failure

Question 16:

    4. Availability Zone

Question 17:

    3. SSH Keys

Question 18:

3. Global Infrastructure

Question 19:

2. Amazon S3

Question 20:

1. Consolidated Billing

Conclusion

The AWS Certified Cloud Practitioner is for anyone looking to gain knowledge and a clear understanding of AWS and cloud computing concepts. The AWS CCP course is a beginner to intermediate course which stands as a foundation to learning the more advanced AWS solutions.

By the time the student has completed this course, they should have an understanding of what cloud computing is, how AWS works, and what the key services and characteristics of the platform are.

If you have successfully worked your way through this guide and managed to successfully complete the test questions, you should be well-versed on what to expect from the certification exams. It is also highly recommended that you use the reference links to each of the testing facilities to ensure you are fully prepared for the CCP examination.

Good luck, stay confident, and positive.

References

AWS Certified Cloud Practitioner (CLF-C01) Exam Guide [PDF File]. (n.d.). AWS Training. https://d1.awsstatic.com/training-and-certification/docs-cloud-practitioner/AWS-Certified-Cloud-Practitioner_Exam-Guide.pdf

AWS Cloud Practitioner Essentials (Second Edition). (n.d.). AWS Training. https://www.aws.training/

AWS White papers & Guides. (n.d.). AWS Training. https://aws.amazon.com/whitepapers/?whitepapers-main.sort-by=item.additionalFields.sortDate&whitepapers-main.sort-order=desc

The 4 Methods of Cloud Deployment. (2017, July 18). LinkedIn. https://www.linkedin.com/pulse/4-methods-cloud-deployment-jim-barnish-jr-/

www.ingramcontent.com/pod-product-compliance
Lightning Source LLC
LaVergne TN
LVHW051744050326
832903LV00029B/2705